365 Fan

Your Daily I

Di

Introduction	4
January: Historical Events and Figures	5
February: Science and Technology	13
March: The Animal Kingdom	21
April: Fun Pop Culture	29
May: The Human Body	37
June: Space and Astronomy	45
July: Nature and the Environment	53
August: Food and Drink	61
September: Geography and Travel	69
October: Mysteries and Oddities	77
November: Inventions and Discoveries	86
December: Holidays and Traditions	95
In Conclusion	104
Discover More with Our Exclusive Book Bundles!	106
Want a Sneak Preview?	109
Claim Your FREE Book!	110
About the Author	111

365 Fantastic Facts!
Your Daily Dose of Delightful Discoveries

Part of the Daily Laugh and Learn Series

Copyright © 2024 Dan Furze
All rights reserved.

The author asserts the moral right to be identified as the creator of this work. No part of this publication may be reproduced, distributed, or transmitted in any form or by any means, including photocopying, recording, or other electronic or mechanical methods, without the prior written permission of the author, except in the case of brief quotations embodied in reviews or critical articles and certain other noncommercial uses permitted by copyright law. For permission requests, contact the author at dan@furze.media.

This book contains research from publicly available sources, and while every effort has been made to ensure the accuracy of the information presented, the author does not claim ownership of facts, data, or publicly available knowledge. All interpretations, conclusions, and commentary are the original work of the author.

ISBN: 9798343327212
First Edition: 2024
Published by Dan Furze

Introduction

Welcome to 365 Fantastic Facts, your year-long journey through the wonders of the world. Whether you're a trivia lover, a curious soul, or someone who enjoys a little spark of knowledge each day, this book is your daily ticket to a fascinating discovery.

Every day of the year, you'll be treated to a fact that's not just interesting, but guaranteed to give you a delightful "aha!" moment. From the deep mysteries of space to the quirks of pop culture, and from the extraordinary world of animals to the marvels of human invention, there's something here for everyone. Each fact is a bite-sized nugget of knowledge, designed to surprise, inform, and maybe even inspire.

The book is organized into monthly themes, each focusing on a different area of interest. January begins with a trip through history, shedding light on forgotten figures and monumental events. As the year unfolds, we'll journey through science, animals, food, and even the mysteries of the universe. By December, we'll be celebrating with facts about holidays and traditions from around the world.

Our goal? To remind you that the world is full of wonder. There's always something new to learn, something surprising waiting around the corner. So whether you're flipping through the pages each morning with your coffee or saving up for a binge-read, we hope these facts will bring a little extra curiosity into your day.

Let's dive into 365 fantastic discoveries and make every day a little more fascinating!

January: Historical Events and Figures

We're kicking off the year with a dive into the quirkiest corners of history. Forget the textbook version—this month we're unearthing strange and fascinating tidbits about the past that you probably won't hear in school.

From peculiar personalities to bizarre events that shaped the world in unexpected ways, these facts prove that history is far more than dates and battles—it's full of surprises, too!

Buckle up for a journey through the weird, wonderful, and wildly unexpected moments of history.

January 1st / Day 1

When Pope Gregory IX issued a decree in the 1230s condemning cats as instruments of Satan, it indirectly led to a massive increase in the rat population, which some historians believe contributed to the spread of the Black Death.

January 2nd / Day 2

In 1920, Babe Ruth's home run hit shattered not just a baseball record, but also a dentist's window across the street, earning him free dental care for life!

January 3rd / Day 3

President Andrew Jackson once parroted back an expletive-filled tirade his pet parrot had learned—so much so that the bird had to be removed from Jackson's funeral.

January 4th / Day 4

Napoleon Bonaparte wasn't particularly short for his time. He was about 5'6"—the average height for a Frenchman in the early 1800s. So much for that "Napoleon complex" myth!

January 5th / Day 5

The Leaning Tower of Pisa was never intended to lean! It started tilting during construction in the 12th century due to poor foundation work, and it just kept leaning ever since.

January 6th / Day 6

Albert Einstein's brain was stolen after his death in 1955. A pathologist at Princeton kept it for decades, cutting it into pieces and storing it in jars!

January 7th / Day 7

In 1799, the French army accidentally discovered the Rosetta Stone while building a fort in Egypt. Talk about stumbling upon world-changing history by chance!

January 8th / Day 8

During the Cold War, the CIA tried to spy on the Kremlin and Soviet embassies by using cats outfitted with recording devices. The project was abandoned after the first mission when the "spy cat" ran into traffic.

January 9th / Day 9

Thomas Edison didn't invent the lightbulb—he improved upon it. The original bulb design was created by British inventor Humphry Davy decades earlier.

January 10th / Day 10

During World War II, the British Secret Service secretly made maps for prisoners of war that were hidden inside Monopoly boards, along with real money and tools for escape.

January 11th / Day 11

Napoleon Bonaparte was once attacked by a horde of rabbits. After a hunting party in 1807, the rabbits turned on him when their hunger outmatched their fear!

January 12th / Day 12

In 1838, General Antonio López de Santa Anna, the Mexican president, held a full state funeral for his amputated leg, complete with military honors.

January 13th / Day 13

Cleopatra used to dissolve pearls in vinegar and drink them to flaunt her wealth and sophistication—talk about a pricey cocktail!

January 14th / Day 14

King George I of England was actually German and spoke very little English when he took the throne in 1714. This didn't stop him from ruling for 13 years.

January 15th / Day 15

Albert Einstein was offered the presidency of Israel in 1952 but declined, saying he had "neither the natural aptitude nor the experience to deal with human beings."

January 16th / Day 16

In 1518, residents of Strasbourg, France, experienced a "dancing plague," where people danced uncontrollably for days. Some literally danced themselves to death!

January 17th / Day 17

During World War II, British soldiers were given carrots to improve their night vision—leading to the myth that eating carrots helps you see in the dark.

January 18th / Day 18

In the 17th century, the Dutch went through a period known as "Tulip Mania," where single tulip bulbs were sold for more than 10 times the annual salary of a skilled worker!

January 19th / Day 19

In 1923, jockey Frank Hayes won a horse race in New York despite being dead. He suffered a heart attack mid-race but remained in the saddle as his horse crossed the finish line first.

January 20th / Day 20

The famous outlaw Jesse James's first bank robbery netted him just $15, which would be worth less than $300 today—not quite the haul you'd expect for a legendary outlaw.

January 21st / Day 21

King Tutankhamun's tomb, discovered in 1922, contained over 5,000 treasures, including a dagger made from a meteorite. Ancient Egyptians apparently had an affinity for space bling!

January 22nd / Day 22

President John Quincy Adams loved swimming in the Potomac River—naked. In fact, a female journalist once interviewed him by sitting on his clothes until he agreed to answer her questions!

January 23rd / Day 23

In 1917, the British royal family changed their last name from Saxe-Coburg and Gotha to Windsor to sound less German during World War I. "House of Windsor" certainly rolls off the tongue a bit better!

January 24th / Day 24

The Library of Congress is the largest library in the world, but it didn't start that way—it was founded with a modest collection of 740 books, mostly from Thomas Jefferson's personal library.

January 25th / Day 25

Queen Elizabeth II technically owned all the unmarked mute swans in the UK. Swans were originally considered royal property as far back as the 12th century.

January 26th / Day 26

In 1986, Soviet cosmonaut Valentin Lebedev was reprimanded for playing too much chess aboard the Salyut 7 space station during his 211-day mission.

January 27th / Day 27

The first "television dinner" was actually invented in 1953 by Swanson as a way to deal with 520,000 pounds of leftover Thanksgiving turkey. Talk about a creative solution to leftovers!

January 28th / Day 28

The Colosseum in Rome was once flooded for mock naval battles. The arena floor could be filled with water to recreate sea skirmishes for a bloodthirsty audience.

January 29th / Day 29

Before alarm clocks, people hired "knocker-uppers" to wake them by tapping on their windows with long sticks. No snooze button for these early risers!

January 30th / Day 30

In ancient Rome, the punishment for killing your father was being sewn into a sack with a dog, a rooster, a monkey, and a snake, and then thrown into a river. Tough family love!

January 31st / Day 31

The world's shortest war took place in 1896 between Britain and Zanzibar. It lasted a mere 38 minutes before Zanzibar surrendered. Blink and you missed it!

February: Science and Technology

February is all about the mind-blowing wonders of science and the dazzling innovations of technology.

From accidental inventions that changed the world to bizarre scientific discoveries that make you question reality, this month is packed with fascinating facts that showcase the brilliance—and sometimes quirkiness—of human achievement.

Prepare to explore the cutting edge, the strange, and the downright genius as we delve into the world of science and tech!

February 1st / Day 32

In 1943, a Swedish engineer accidentally invented the pacemaker while working on a completely different project—a heart rate recorder. Talk about a life-saving detour!

February 2nd / Day 33

The first webcam ever was created at Cambridge University to monitor a coffee pot. Yes, it was literally set up so scientists could avoid pointless trips to an empty coffee machine!

February 3rd / Day 34

A bolt of lightning contains enough energy to toast 100,000 slices of bread. That's one shocking way to get breakfast done fast!

February 4th / Day 35

Astronauts aboard the International Space Station grow radishes in space. Why? Because radishes grow quickly and are easy to study in microgravity. Plus, space salads are pretty cool.

February 5th / Day 36

In the 1960s, IBM created the first artificial intelligence to win a chess game—except the computer wasn't actually that smart. It won because the opponent made an illegal move, which it happened to catch!

February 6th / Day 37

In 2008, physicists successfully created a mini "Big Bang" by colliding particles at nearly the speed of light in the Large Hadron Collider. Luckily, the universe didn't implode!

February 7th / Day 38

A cloud can weigh over a million pounds. The next time you look up at a fluffy cloud, remember—it's not as light as it seems!

February 8th / Day 39

The first email was sent by Ray Tomlinson in 1971. It was a test message, and Tomlinson later admitted he couldn't remember what he had written. Possibly the world's most forgettable "first"!

February 9th / Day 40

Sharks have existed for longer than trees. These ancient predators have been swimming in the oceans for about 400 million years, while trees have been around for a mere 350 million.

February 10th / Day 41

In 1977, the first Star Wars movie used computer-controlled cameras for special effects, an innovation that changed the way films were made forever. The Force of technology was strong with this one.

February 11th / Day 42

The word "robot" comes from the Czech word "robota," meaning forced labor. It first appeared in a 1920 play about a dystopian world where robots rebel against humans.

February 12th / Day 43

In 1992, the Great Moon Hoax convinced many that NASA had found evidence of life on the moon, including plants and animals. Spoiler: It was all made up!

February 13th / Day 44

The longest hiccuping spree lasted 68 years. Charles Osborne started hiccuping in 1922 and didn't stop until 1990, logging around 430 million hiccups during his lifetime.

February 14th / Day 45

The Apollo 11 astronauts couldn't get life insurance before their mission to the moon, so they signed hundreds of autographs in case anything went wrong. Their families would've sold them to cover costs.

February 15th / Day 46

The inventor of the frisbee was turned into a frisbee after he died. Edward "Steady Ed" Headrick's ashes were molded into frisbees, so he could keep flying forever!

February 16th / Day 47

Bananas are technically radioactive because they contain potassium-40, a naturally occurring isotope. Don't worry though—you'd have to eat about 10 million bananas in one sitting for it to harm you!

February 17th / Day 48

The patent for the fire hydrant is unknown because the original patent office building burned down in 1836, destroying the records—including the one for fire hydrants. Oh, the irony!

February 18th / Day 49

The smell of freshly-cut grass is actually a plant distress signal. When grass is injured, it releases a chemical compound to warn surrounding plants of danger—so that "fresh" scent is really a scream for help!

February 19th / Day 50

In 1996, Apple's Power Macintosh 7100 had a secret "Easter egg" sound effect that said, "Welcome to Macintosh... you are standing on my toes!" if you held down certain keys while starting it up.

February 20th / Day 51

The "Ctrl+Alt+Delete" keyboard shortcut was invented by IBM engineer David Bradley as a way to reboot a computer. He claims it became famous because Bill Gates "made it famous."

February 21st / Day 52

Bubble wrap was originally designed to be used as textured wallpaper in the 1960s, but when that idea flopped, it found its calling as protective packaging material.

February 22nd / Day 53

The first-ever computer virus was created in 1983 by a 15-year-old named Rich Skrenta. It was a practical joke virus that would display a poem after infecting the user's system.

February 23rd / Day 54

The inventor of the microwave oven, Percy Spencer, came up with the idea after a chocolate bar melted in his pocket while he was working on a radar device. Sweet inspiration!

February 24th / Day 55

A teaspoon of neutron star material would weigh about 6 billion tons on Earth. So, while you could fit it in a spoon, you definitely wouldn't want to carry it!

February 25th / Day 56

In 1999, NASA's Mars Climate Orbiter disintegrated because engineers used imperial units in some calculations while others used metric, leading to a $125 million mistake. Oops!

February 26th / Day 57

In 2011, IBM's AI program Watson won "Jeopardy!" against two of the greatest human champions. It turns out computers are pretty good at trivia!

February 27th / Day 58

The Eiffel Tower can "grow" by up to 15 centimeters in summer. The metal expands when it heats up, causing the iconic structure to rise and tilt ever so slightly.

February 28th / Day 59

In the 1800s, people believed that chewing gum would stay in your stomach for seven years if swallowed. While it's not advisable to gulp down gum, it certainly doesn't take that long to digest!

February 29th / Leap Year Bonus!

Julius Caesar introduced leap years in 45 BC, but they weren't perfect until 1582, when Pope Gregory XIII fixed the calendar with the Gregorian system we use today. Without this adjustment, our calendars would be way off!

March: The Animal Kingdom

March is all about the wild, wonderful, and sometimes downright weird creatures that inhabit our planet.

From the tiniest critters to the kings of the jungle, the animal kingdom is packed with fascinating behaviors and quirky facts that'll have you looking at our furry, feathered, and scaly friends in a whole new light.

Get ready to be amazed by creatures that defy logic, and prepare for some fun surprises from the most unexpected corners of the animal world!

March 1st / Day 60

A group of flamingos is called a "flamboyance"—a fitting name for some of the flashiest birds around!

March 2nd / Day 61

Sloths only poop once a week, and when they do, they lose up to a third of their body weight. It's like the ultimate diet plan... but not one you'd want to follow!

March 3rd / Day 62

Koalas sleep up to 22 hours a day. These eucalyptus-munching marsupials take being laid-back to a whole new level.

March 4th / Day 63

The male seahorse is the one that gets pregnant and gives birth. In fact, he can carry and deliver up to 2,000 babies at once—talk about multitasking!

March 5th / Day 64

Penguins propose with pebbles! Male penguins search for the perfect pebble to present to their chosen mate, and if the female accepts, it's love at first stone.

March 6th / Day 65

Cows have best friends and get stressed when they're separated. So, next time you see a cow, just know they might be hanging out with their BFF.

March 7th / Day 66

Wombat poop is cube-shaped, and no one knows exactly why. These square droppings help keep their "presents" from rolling away in their hilly habitat.

March 8th / Day 67

Jellyfish have no brain, no heart, and no bones, yet they've been floating around Earth for over 500 million years. They're the ultimate minimalist survivors!

March 9th / Day 68

Male bowerbirds are master decorators. They build elaborate nests and carefully decorate them with colorful objects like berries and bottle caps to attract a mate. Who knew birds could be interior designers?

March 10th / Day 69

The horned lizard can shoot blood from its eyes as a defense mechanism. This surprising trick helps it fend off predators, and probably grosses them out too!

March 11th / Day 70

An octopus can taste with its arms! Each sucker on an octopus's arm is equipped with chemoreceptors, allowing it to taste whatever it touches.

March 12th / Day 71

Tardigrades, also known as water bears, are nearly indestructible. They can survive extreme temperatures, radiation, the vacuum of space, and even being boiled or frozen!

March 13th / Day 72

A shrimp's heart is located in its head. So, when you say something is "all heart," you might be talking about shrimp more than you know!

March 14th / Day 73

Giraffes only need 5 to 30 minutes of sleep in a 24-hour period, often in short naps. With their height, they're always on alert, ready to spot danger.

March 15th / Day 74

Axolotls can regenerate almost any part of their body, including their limbs, heart, and even parts of their brain. They're the real-life superheroes of the animal world!

March 16th / Day 75

Crows are known to hold grudges. They can remember human faces for years and will "tell" other crows if someone has wronged them, spreading the message far and wide!

March 17th / Day 76

Elephants are the only animals that can't jump. But with their size, they don't really need to—gravity keeps them pretty well grounded!

March 18th / Day 77

Ostriches can run faster than horses, reaching speeds of up to 70 kilometers per hour (43 mph). In fact, their two-legged sprint could outrun many predators.

March 19th / Day 78

Dolphins give themselves names. They develop a unique whistle that acts as their personal identification, allowing them to recognize each other in the wild.

March 20th / Day 79

Tigers not only have striped fur, but their skin is striped too. If you shaved one, the stripes would still be there—talk about built-in fashion!

March 21st / Day 80

Pigeons can recognize themselves in a mirror, one of the few species to pass this test of self-awareness. So next time you see a pigeon strutting, it might just be admiring itself!

March 22nd / Day 81

Polar bears have black skin beneath their white fur, which helps them absorb heat from the sun. Their "white" fur is actually translucent, reflecting light and blending with snow.

March 23rd / Day 82

Sea otters hold hands while they sleep to keep from drifting apart. Entire groups, called rafts, can be seen floating together, all holding paws!

March 24th / Day 83

Horses can't vomit. Their digestive systems are designed in a way that prevents regurgitation, so they're quite careful about what they eat.

March 25th / Day 84

Starfish can regenerate lost limbs, and in some cases, a single arm can regenerate into a whole new starfish. Talk about a backup plan!

March 26th / Day 85

Platypuses don't have stomachs. Their esophagus connects directly to their intestines, making their digestive system one of the strangest in the animal kingdom.

March 27th / Day 86

A group of porcupines is called a "prickle." Fitting for animals that carry their own personal set of sharp needles!

March 28th / Day 87

Butterflies taste with their feet. When they land on a plant, they use sensors on their legs to taste the leaves and decide if it's good for laying eggs.

March 29th / Day 88

Female ferrets can die if they don't find a mate. When in heat, their bodies continue to produce high levels of estrogen, which can become toxic if they don't breed.

March 30th / Day 89

A chameleon's tongue is twice the length of its body, and it can shoot it out in less than a second to catch prey. It's the ultimate sticky-tongue grabber!

March 31st / Day 90

Bees can detect bombs. They've been trained to associate the smell of explosives with food and can signal handlers when they've found something suspicious by sticking out their tongues.

April: Fun Pop Culture

April is all about diving into the quirky world of pop culture—movies, music, TV, and all the little-known facts behind your favorite entertainment. Whether it's surprising origins, strange behind-the-scenes moments, or bizarre celebrity trivia, this month will have you looking at pop culture with fresh eyes.

From iconic moments on the big screen to the hidden stories of famous songs, we're pulling back the curtain on some seriously fun facts.

Get ready for a nostalgia-fueled ride through the pop culture you thought you knew!

April 1st / Day 91

The voice of Yoda in Star Wars is performed by Frank Oz, who also voiced Miss Piggy from The Muppets. So, in a way, Yoda and Miss Piggy are one and the same!

April 2nd / Day 92

The original name for the band The Beatles was "The Silver Beetles," a nod to Buddy Holly's band, "The Crickets." Thankfully, they simplified things before taking over the world.

April 3rd / Day 93

The entire movie Clerks was filmed for less than $28,000, and Kevin Smith financed it by maxing out his credit cards. Sometimes, great things start with a lot of debt!

April 4th / Day 94

Before settling on Breaking Bad, creator Vince Gilligan considered calling the show Meth, which would've been... pretty blunt, to say the least.

April 5th / Day 95

In the movie Pulp Fiction, John Travolta's character famously dances at Jack Rabbit Slim's. The twist? Travolta was once a professional dancer before his acting career took off!

April 6th / Day 96

The world's first music video was Queen's Bohemian Rhapsody, created in 1975 to promote the song. Little did they know, they were kickstarting a whole new era of music promotion.

April 7th / Day 97

The first video ever uploaded to YouTube was called "Me at the zoo," posted by co-founder Jawed Karim in 2005. It's 19 seconds of him talking about elephants.

April 8th / Day 98

In The Matrix, the iconic "rain" of green code was actually created from symbols in a Japanese sushi recipe. Who knew computer code could be so delicious?

April 9th / Day 99

Elvis Presley was naturally blonde but dyed his hair jet black to create his signature look. He even used shoe polish to touch it up when dye wasn't available!

April 10th / Day 100

The Terminator franchise's famous line "I'll be back" was almost "I'll come back." Arnold Schwarzenegger insisted on changing it because he felt it sounded more robotic.

April 11th / Day 101

The song "Happy Birthday to You" was once copyrighted, and its use in movies or TV required paying royalties. It wasn't until 2016 that the song entered the public domain.

April 12th / Day 102

Mickey Mouse was the first animated character to get a star on the Hollywood Walk of Fame, earning his place in 1978. That mouse sure knows how to make history!

April 13th / Day 103

In the movie Psycho, Alfred Hitchcock used chocolate syrup for the infamous shower scene. It gave the perfect consistency and appearance of blood in black-and-white film.

April 14th / Day 104

The original title for the movie Back to the Future was Spaceman from Pluto, but producers wisely thought the current title would be more timeless.

April 15th / Day 105

In Friends, all six main cast members were originally paid $22,500 per episode. By the final season, they each made $1 million per episode. That's some serious friendship goals!

April 16th / Day 106

The famous Wilhelm Scream, a stock sound effect of a man screaming, has been used in over 400 movies, including Star Wars, Indiana Jones, and Toy Story. It's Hollywood's inside joke!

April 17th / Day 107

The iconic James Bond theme song was originally written for a completely different movie called A House for Mr. Biswas. Talk about a theme finding its true home.

April 18th / Day 108

The Simpsons family was designed with such distinct silhouettes that they would be recognizable even in shadow. Creator Matt Groening wanted them to stand out instantly.

April 19th / Day 109

In Jurassic Park, the sound of the velociraptors communicating was made by tortoises mating. Movie magic sure can be strange!

April 20th / Day 110

The character of Chewbacca in Star Wars was inspired by George Lucas's dog, Indiana, a large Alaskan Malamute. In fact, Indiana also inspired the name of Lucas's other famous character, Indiana Jones!

April 21st / Day 111

The famous line "You're gonna need a bigger boat" from Jaws was ad-libbed by Roy Scheider. It wasn't in the script, but it became one of the most iconic lines in movie history.

April 22nd / Day 112

In Toy Story, Buzz Lightyear was originally going to be named "Lunar Larry." The change to Buzz was made as a tribute to astronaut Buzz Aldrin.

April 23rd / Day 113

David Bowie's iconic different-colored eyes were the result of a fistfight as a teenager. A punch to his eye permanently damaged the pupil, giving it its distinct appearance.

April 24th / Day 114

The title of the movie E.T. the Extra-Terrestrial was originally just "E.T. and Me." It was changed to make the film sound more mysterious and intriguing.

April 25th / Day 115

The voice of Shrek was originally recorded by Chris Farley before his passing, and Mike Myers re-recorded the lines. Myers even decided to give Shrek his signature Scottish accent later in the process.

April 26th / Day 116

In The Dark Knight, Heath Ledger designed the Joker's iconic makeup himself, using cheap drugstore products. He wanted it to look like the Joker did his own makeup on the fly.

April 27th / Day 117

Michael Jackson's famous moonwalk debuted during a performance of "Billie Jean" in 1983, but the move itself was inspired by street dancers Jackson saw in Los Angeles.

April 28th / Day 118

The famous opening crawl of Star Wars was created using practical effects, with the text printed on paper and filmed as it scrolled in front of the camera.

April 29th / Day 119

In Harry Potter, the actor who played Moaning Myrtle, Shirley Henderson, was 37 years old when she portrayed the ghost of a teenage girl. She's one of the oldest actors to play a Hogwarts student!

April 30th / Day 120

The entire movie Paranormal Activity was made for just $15,000, but it went on to gross nearly $200 million worldwide, making it one of the most profitable movies ever made!

May: The Human Body

May is all about the weird and wonderful workings of the human body. From the everyday miracles that keep us ticking to the bizarre quirks that make us unique, this month will dive into fascinating facts about what goes on beneath the skin.

Our bodies are more than just muscle and bone—they're packed with hidden talents, strange abilities, and plenty of surprises.

Get ready to explore the human body like never before and discover just how incredible (and sometimes odd) we really are!

May 1st / Day 121

Your stomach gets a new lining every three to four days to prevent it from digesting itself. Without this regular regeneration, stomach acid would eat right through it!

May 2nd / Day 122

Humans are the only animals that blush. It's a reaction controlled by the same system that triggers the fight-or-flight response—your body's way of admitting, "Yep, I'm embarrassed!"

May 3rd / Day 123

You produce about 1 to 1.5 liters of saliva each day—enough to fill two medium-sized soda bottles. Most of it is swallowed without you even noticing.

May 4th / Day 124

The human nose can detect over 1 trillion different scents, far more than previously thought. Your nose is basically a finely tuned scent-detecting machine!

May 5th / Day 125

Your bones are about five times stronger than steel. Pound for pound, human bone can bear nearly as much pressure as cast iron.

May 6th / Day 126

Your ears and nose never stop growing. While your body may stop getting taller, cartilage continues to grow throughout your life, giving you bigger ears and nose as you age.

May 7th / Day 127

The acid in your stomach is strong enough to dissolve razor blades. While you should never test this out, it shows just how powerful your digestive juices really are!

May 8th / Day 128

When you take a step, you use up to 200 muscles. Walking is much more of a full-body workout than it seems, even if you're just strolling through the park.

May 9th / Day 129

Humans shed about 600,000 particles of skin every hour. By the end of a year, you'll have shed about 3.6 kilograms (8 pounds) of dead skin—basically an entire layer of yourself!

May 10th / Day 130

You can't tickle yourself. Your brain knows it's coming and cancels out the sensation. It's one of the ways your brain protects you from unnecessary sensory overload.

May 11th / Day 131

Your brain uses the same amount of power as a 10-watt light bulb. Despite weighing only about 2% of your body weight, it consumes around 20% of your energy!

May 12th / Day 132

The human body contains around 37 trillion cells. If you could line up all your cells end to end, they would stretch around the Earth over 200 times!

May 13th / Day 133

Goosebumps are an evolutionary leftover from when our ancestors had more body hair. The raised hairs made them appear larger when threatened—today, it's just our body's quirky reaction to cold or fear.

May 14th / Day 134

Your eyes blink about 15 to 20 times per minute, which means you blink over 28,000 times a day. That's roughly 10% of your waking hours spent blinking!

May 15th / Day 135

Your liver can regenerate itself. It's the only organ in the human body that can completely grow back even if up to 75% of it is removed.

May 16th / Day 136

Humans are the best long-distance runners on Earth. Our ability to sweat and regulate body heat allows us to outrun almost any animal over long distances.

May 17th / Day 137

You can see ultraviolet light, but it's filtered out by the lenses of your eyes. After cataract surgery, some patients report seeing UV light, making colors appear even more vivid.

May 18th / Day 138

Your tongue is made up of eight interlocking muscles, similar in structure to an elephant's trunk or an octopus's tentacle. It's also the only muscle that doesn't connect to a bone at both ends.

May 19th / Day 139

You lose about 30,000 to 40,000 skin cells every minute. Most of the dust in your house is made up of tiny flakes of your dead skin cells. Talk about leaving a mark!

May 20th / Day 140

Your body has enough iron in it to make a small nail. Most of this iron is in your blood, playing a crucial role in transporting oxygen throughout your body.

May 21st / Day 141

The average human body has about 100,000 kilometers (62,000 miles) of blood vessels. That's enough to circle the Earth over two times!

May 22nd / Day 142

When you listen to music, your heartbeat syncs up with the rhythm. So next time you feel that beat, remember your heart's dancing along with you!

May 23rd / Day 143

The human body emits a small amount of visible light, but it's 1,000 times weaker than what our eyes can detect. Essentially, you glow in the dark, but not quite like a firefly.

May 24th / Day 144

Yawning cools your brain. Scientists believe yawning helps regulate the temperature of your brain, especially when it's overheating or under strain.

May 25th / Day 145

Your feet have around 250,000 sweat glands. They can produce up to half a liter (about a pint) of sweat in a single day, so blame those glands next time your feet get sweaty!

May 26th / Day 146

Your body replaces about 98% of its atoms every year. So, in a sense, you're practically a new person every 365 days!

May 27th / Day 147

You can't breathe and swallow at the same time. The body's design prevents these two actions from happening simultaneously—try it, you'll see!

May 28th / Day 148

If the human eye were a digital camera, it would have a resolution of 576 megapixels. That's a lot sharper than the latest smartphones!

May 29th / Day 149

Your teeth are the only part of your body that can't heal themselves. Once damaged, they need outside help—hence the importance of regular dentist visits!

May 30th / Day 150

The left side of your body is controlled by the right side of your brain, and vice versa. So, technically, you're always a little bit cross-wired!

May 31st / Day 151

The "butterflies" you feel in your stomach when you're nervous are caused by a surge of adrenaline. Your body diverts blood away from your digestive system, causing that fluttery feeling.

June: Space and Astronomy

June takes us beyond our world and into the cosmos! This month, we're exploring the vast mysteries of space, where the wonders of planets, stars, black holes, and galaxies await.

From mind-bending facts about the infinite universe to the amazing feats of human space exploration, we're setting our sights on the stars—and beyond. Buckle up for a journey through space that's as fascinating as it is infinite.

Prepare for liftoff into the strange, beautiful, and downright awe-inspiring universe!

June 1st / Day 152

A day on Venus is longer than a year on Venus. It takes the planet 243 Earth days to rotate once on its axis, but only 225 Earth days to orbit the Sun.

June 2nd / Day 153

There are more stars in the universe than grains of sand on all the beaches on Earth. The universe holds roughly 1 septillion stars—that's a 1 followed by 24 zeros!

June 3rd / Day 154

The largest volcano in the solar system is Olympus Mons on Mars. It's about three times the height of Mount Everest and is so big that it could cover the entire state of New Mexico!

June 4th / Day 155

Neutron stars are so dense that just a sugar-cube-sized amount of their matter would weigh about 1 billion tons. That's heavier than all the cars on Earth combined.

June 5th / Day 156

Space is completely silent because there's no atmosphere to carry sound. So, if you scream in space, nobody can hear you—but it's probably better to keep calm anyway!

June 6th / Day 157

The Sun makes up 99.86% of the mass in our solar system. Everything else—planets, moons, asteroids, and comets—account for just a tiny fraction of the solar system's mass.

June 7th / Day 158

On Saturn's moon Titan, it rains methane instead of water. Methane rivers and lakes dot its surface, making it one of the most Earth-like places in our solar system—but with a much colder twist.

June 8th / Day 159

A day on the International Space Station lasts about 90 minutes, meaning astronauts on board experience 16 sunrises and sunsets every single day!

June 9th / Day 160

The footprints left by astronauts on the Moon will stay there for millions of years. Without wind or water to erode them, they're frozen in time on the lunar surface.

June 10th / Day 161

If two pieces of the same metal touch in space, they will fuse together permanently. This is called cold welding, and it happens because there's no air or moisture to keep the metal atoms apart.

June 11th / Day 162

Jupiter's Great Red Spot is a massive storm that has been raging for at least 350 years. It's so large that three Earths could fit inside it!

June 12th / Day 163

There's a planet called 55 Cancri e where it rains diamonds. This exoplanet is so rich in carbon that scientists believe its interior is made of diamond and graphite.

June 13th / Day 164

A single day on Mercury lasts about 59 Earth days, but its year—one full orbit around the Sun—is just 88 Earth days long.

June 14th / Day 165

There's a hexagonal storm on Saturn's north pole that's over twice the size of Earth. It's been raging for decades, and scientists are still trying to figure out exactly why it's hexagon-shaped!

June 15th / Day 166

If you could travel at the speed of light, it would still take you over four years to reach the nearest star, Proxima Centauri, which is about 4.24 light-years away.

June 16th / Day 167

There's a giant cloud of alcohol in space, about 1,000 times the diameter of our solar system. This space booze cloud is made of ethanol and could make 400 trillion trillion pints of beer!

June 17th / Day 168

The hottest planet in our solar system isn't Mercury, even though it's closest to the Sun—it's Venus, with surface temperatures reaching a scorching 475°C (900°F).

June 18th / Day 169

Mars has the largest dust storms in the solar system, sometimes covering the entire planet for months. These storms are so intense they can be seen from Earth with telescopes.

June 19th / Day 170

Uranus rotates on its side, making it the only planet in the solar system to do so. Scientists think it was knocked over by a collision with another celestial object billions of years ago.

June 20th / Day 171

Black holes aren't empty voids—they're incredibly dense objects with gravity so strong that not even light can escape. If you fell into one, you'd be stretched out like spaghetti!

June 21st / Day 172

A teaspoon of matter from a neutron star would weigh about 6 billion tons. That's equivalent to the weight of Mount Everest packed into a tiny spoon!

June 22nd / Day 173

Saturn's rings are made mostly of ice and rock, and they can be as thin as just 10 meters in some places, even though they stretch over 280,000 kilometers wide.

June 23rd / Day 174

On Pluto, a year lasts 248 Earth years, but its day is only about 6.4 Earth days long. If you could visit, you'd experience a lot of slow, dark days.

June 24th / Day 175

The largest canyon in the solar system, Valles Marineris on Mars, is about 10 times longer and five times deeper than the Grand Canyon, stretching over 4,000 kilometers.

June 25th / Day 176

The universe is expanding, and it's speeding up! Galaxies are moving away from each other faster and faster, and scientists are still trying to figure out why.

June 26th / Day 177

It takes sunlight about 8 minutes and 20 seconds to reach Earth from the Sun. So when you look at the Sun, you're actually seeing it as it was 8 minutes ago.

June 27th / Day 178

The largest star known, UY Scuti, is so massive that if it were placed in the center of our solar system, its outer surface would extend beyond Jupiter's orbit.

June 28th / Day 179

If you were on the Moon, your weight would be about one-sixth of what it is on Earth. That's because the Moon's gravity is much weaker—time to test out your moon jumps!

June 29th / Day 180

A year on Neptune lasts 165 Earth years. Since its discovery in 1846, Neptune has only completed one full orbit around the Sun.

June 30th / Day 181

There's a "super-Earth" exoplanet, Gliese 581d, which may be one of the most Earth-like planets discovered. It's in the "habitable zone," where liquid water could exist—but it's 20 light-years away!

July: Nature and the Environment

This month, we're turning our attention to the incredible world of nature and the environment.

From the dense rainforests to the deepest oceans, the Earth is home to amazing ecosystems, strange plants, and mind-boggling natural phenomena. July is all about celebrating the wonders of the natural world, learning more about how it works, and uncovering some of the most bizarre and fascinating facts about our planet.

Get ready to dive into the wild side of nature!

July 1st / Day 183

Bananas are technically berries, but strawberries aren't! Botanically, bananas meet the criteria for berries, while strawberries belong in a different category.

July 2nd / Day 183

Ants are the longest-living insects. Some queen ants can live up to 30 years, making them the elders of the insect kingdom.

July 3rd / Day 184

The Amazon Rainforest produces 20% of the world's oxygen, earning it the nickname "the lungs of the Earth." It's also home to around 390 billion individual trees!

July 4th / Day 185

There's a type of jellyfish called Turritopsis dohrnii that is biologically immortal. It can revert to its juvenile form after reaching adulthood, effectively avoiding death.

July 5th / Day 186

A single tree can absorb up to 22 kilograms (48 pounds) of carbon dioxide each year, making forests essential for combating climate change.

July 6th / Day 187

There are more trees on Earth than stars in the Milky Way galaxy. Estimates suggest there are over 3 trillion trees, compared to around 100 billion stars in our galaxy.

July 7th / Day 188

The Great Barrier Reef is the largest living structure on Earth, stretching over 2,300 kilometers. It's so vast that it can be seen from space.

July 8th / Day 189

Some species of bamboo can grow up to 91 centimeters (35 inches) in a single day. It's one of the fastest-growing plants on the planet!

July 9th / Day 190

There are more species of fish in the Amazon River than in the entire Atlantic Ocean. This river is home to a staggering diversity of aquatic life.

July 10th / Day 191

The Sahara Desert is actually growing. It has expanded by about 10% over the last century, due to a combination of natural climate cycles and human activity.

July 11th / Day 192

The giant sequoia is the largest tree species on Earth, with some trees reaching a height of over 90 meters (300 feet) and weighing more than 2.7 million kilograms (6 million pounds).

July 12th / Day 193

The coldest temperature ever recorded on Earth was -128.6°F (-89.2°C) at the Soviet Union's Vostok Station in Antarctica on July 21, 1983.

July 13th / Day 194

The blue whale is the largest animal ever known to have lived, reaching lengths of up to 30 meters (100 feet) and weighing as much as 150 tons—more than the largest dinosaurs.

July 14th / Day 195

Pineapple plants take about two years to produce a single pineapple. It's a slow-growing fruit that requires patience but rewards with tropical sweetness.

July 15th / Day 196

There are more microorganisms in a teaspoon of soil than there are people on Earth. A single gram of soil can contain billions of bacteria, fungi, and other tiny organisms.

July 16th / Day 197

Male seahorses are the ones who carry and give birth to the babies. After the female deposits her eggs into the male's pouch, he fertilizes and nurtures them until they're born.

July 17th / Day 198

Earth is hit by lightning about 100 times per second, totaling around 8.6 million lightning strikes per day. Thunderstorms are constantly lighting up the planet!

July 18th / Day 199

The ocean contains more historical artifacts than all the museums in the world combined. Much of the Earth's history lies beneath the waves, waiting to be discovered.

July 19th / Day 200

About 75% of the world's fresh water is stored in glaciers. These massive ice formations play a crucial role in regulating the Earth's climate.

July 20th / Day 201

The world's largest living organism is a fungal colony in Oregon's Malheur National Forest. It covers over 2,300 acres and is estimated to be thousands of years old.

July 21st / Day 202

A single honeybee will only produce about 1/12th of a teaspoon of honey in its entire lifetime. It takes thousands of bees to create enough honey to fill just one jar!

July 22nd / Day 203

The Dead Sea is so salty that you can float effortlessly on its surface. Its salt content is around 10 times higher than most oceans, making it nearly impossible to sink.

July 23rd / Day 204

The Amazon River is so vast that during the wet season, it can stretch up to 30 miles wide. It holds more water than the next seven largest rivers combined.

July 24th / Day 205

Sloths move so slowly that algae can grow on their fur. This green tint helps them camouflage in the trees, providing extra protection from predators.

July 25th / Day 206

There's a lake in Australia called Lake Hillier that is naturally bright pink. Scientists believe the unique color is due to the presence of algae and bacteria in the water.

July 26th / Day 207

The Monarch butterfly migrates up to 4,800 kilometers (3,000 miles) from Canada to Mexico each year, making it one of the longest migrations in the insect world.

July 27th / Day 208

The deepest part of the ocean, the Mariana Trench, is more than 11 kilometers (7 miles) deep. If Mount Everest were placed inside it, the peak would still be over 2,000 meters underwater.

July 28th / Day 209

There are more species of beetles on Earth than any other animal. With over 350,000 known species, beetles account for nearly 40% of all known insects.

July 29th / Day 210

The oldest known tree in the world is a bristlecone pine in California that is over 4,800 years old. This ancient tree has lived through countless historical events.

July 30th / Day 211

Around 80% of the Earth's species remain undiscovered. The vast majority of life on the planet has yet to be identified, with new species being discovered regularly.

July 31st / Day 212

The Earth's magnetic field is what protects us from harmful solar radiation. Without it, life as we know it would be exposed to deadly solar winds, making the planet uninhabitable.

August: Food and Drink

August is a feast for the senses! This month, we're diving into the deliciously fascinating world of food and drink. From strange culinary traditions to mind-boggling facts about the foods we eat every day, this chapter will take you on a flavorful journey through the history, science, and sheer fun of what we put on our plates and in our glasses. Whether it's bizarre food origins, surprising nutritional tidbits, or culinary customs from around the globe, prepare to have your appetite for knowledge satisfied!

August 1st / Day 213

Ketchup was once sold as medicine. In the early 19th century, it was believed to cure ailments like indigestion. Tomato pills were even made and marketed as a remedy!

August 2nd / Day 214

Honey never spoils. Archaeologists have found pots of honey in ancient Egyptian tombs that are over 3,000 years old and still perfectly edible.

August 3rd / Day 215

The most expensive coffee in the world, kopi luwak, is made from coffee beans that have been eaten and passed through the digestive system of a civet, a small mammal from Southeast Asia.

August 4th / Day 216

Pineapples were once so rare and expensive that they were considered a symbol of wealth and luxury. People even rented them to display at parties!

August 5th / Day 217

Apples are more effective at waking you up in the morning than coffee. Their natural sugars and vitamins give you an energy boost without the caffeine crash.

August 6th / Day 218

The holes in Swiss cheese are caused by bacteria releasing gas as they eat through the milk, creating bubbles that eventually turn into the cheese's signature holes.

August 7th / Day 219

Water makes up about 90% of a cucumber. That's why they're so refreshing and hydrating—essentially a crunchy way to stay hydrated!

August 8th / Day 220

Potatoes were the first vegetable to be grown in space. NASA successfully grew spuds aboard the Space Shuttle Columbia in 1995.

August 9th / Day 221

Chocolate was once used as currency. The ancient Maya and Aztec civilizations valued cacao beans so highly that they were often traded and used to pay taxes.

August 10th / Day 222

Carrots were originally purple. Orange carrots didn't appear until the 17th century when Dutch farmers selectively bred them as a tribute to the royal family, the House of Orange.

August 11th / Day 223

The world's most stolen food is cheese! About 4% of the cheese produced globally is stolen, making it the most pilfered food on the planet.

August 12th / Day 224

Popsicles were invented by an 11-year-old by accident in 1905. Frank Epperson left a cup of soda with a stirring stick outside on a cold night, and when he found it frozen the next morning, the popsicle was born!

August 13th / Day 225

Nutmeg can be toxic if consumed in large quantities. Eating too much of this common spice can lead to hallucinations, nausea, and even poisoning.

August 14th / Day 226

The Caesar salad wasn't named after Julius Caesar. It was actually created by a chef named Caesar Cardini in the 1920s at his restaurant in Tijuana, Mexico.

August 15th / Day 227

Peanuts aren't nuts at all—they're legumes, like beans and lentils. True nuts grow on trees, while peanuts grow underground.

August 16th / Day 228

Ripe cranberries bounce like rubber balls. This peculiar trait is why they're sometimes called "bounceberries," and it's a key factor in harvesting methods.

August 17th / Day 229

It takes about 2,000 flowers for bees to make just one tablespoon of honey. Bees work tirelessly to produce the golden sweetener we enjoy every day.

August 18th / Day 230

The word "toast," as in giving a toast at a celebration, comes from an old tradition of putting spiced toast into drinks like wine for flavor. The act of raising a glass became associated with toasting the bread.

August 19th / Day 231

Fortune cookies aren't actually from China. They were invented in the United States, likely by a Japanese-American baker in California in the early 20th century.

August 20th / Day 232

Bubblegum is pink because the inventor, Walter Diemer, only had pink food coloring on hand when he made the first successful batch of gum in 1928. The color stuck!

August 21st / Day 233

Avocados were once called "alligator pears" due to their bumpy, green skin. Despite their popularity now, they were considered a luxury in the U.S. until the 1950s.

August 22nd / Day 234

The most expensive pizza in the world costs $12,000. It's topped with lobster, caviar, buffalo mozzarella, and 24-carat gold flakes, and takes 72 hours to prepare.

August 23rd / Day 235

French fries originated in Belgium, not France. American soldiers stationed in Belgium during World War I tasted them and, because the Belgian army spoke French, started calling them "French" fries.

August 24th / Day 236

One of the most expensive meats in the world is Wagyu beef, which comes from a special breed of Japanese cattle. The cows are known to be pampered with massages and fed beer!

August 25th / Day 237

The famous sandwich was named after John Montagu, the 4th Earl of Sandwich, who ordered his meal between two slices of bread so he could keep playing cards without greasy fingers.

August 26th / Day 238

The durian, known as the "king of fruits" in Southeast Asia, is infamous for its strong odor, which has been described as a mix of rotten onions, turpentine, and raw sewage.

August 27th / Day 239

Almonds are seeds, not nuts. They're the seeds of the almond tree, which is closely related to peaches, cherries, and apricots.

August 28th / Day 240

The longest noodle ever made measured 3,084 meters (10,119 feet) and was created in China in 2017. That's more than 10 times the height of the Empire State Building!

August 29th / Day 241

During the Middle Ages, spices like black pepper were so valuable they were used as currency. Peppercorns were often accepted as payment for rent and taxes.

August 30th / Day 242

The first chocolate bar was invented in 1847 by a British chocolatier named Joseph Fry, who discovered that combining cocoa butter with cocoa powder and sugar produced a solid bar.

August 31st / Day 243

The world's oldest known recipe is a 4,000-year-old beer recipe from ancient Mesopotamia. It was found on a clay tablet and is one of the earliest examples of written culinary instructions.

September: Geography and Travel

September takes us on a journey around the world! This month is dedicated to exploring the most fascinating places, cultures, and geographical wonders of our planet. From hidden travel gems to mind-blowing facts about countries, cities, and natural landmarks, we'll dive into the diverse and intriguing landscapes that make Earth so unique.

Whether you're an armchair traveler or a globetrotter, these facts will fuel your wanderlust and deepen your appreciation for the incredible world we live in.

Grab your passport—it's time to explore!

September 1st / Day 244

Canada has the longest coastline in the world, stretching over 202,080 kilometers. If you tried to walk its length, it would take more than 30 years without stopping!

September 2nd / Day 245

Iceland is the only country in the world that has no mosquitoes. Thanks to its cold climate and lack of standing water, the pesky insects can't survive there.

September 3rd / Day 246

The Sahara Desert wasn't always a desert. Around 6,000 years ago, it was a lush, green region with lakes and rivers, supporting a wide variety of wildlife.

September 4th / Day 247

Russia is so large that it spans 11 time zones. If you traveled from one end of the country to the other, you'd experience nearly half of the world's time zones in a single journey.

September 5th / Day 248

There's a beach in the Maldives called "Vaadhoo Beach" where the water glows at night. This natural phenomenon, known as bioluminescence, is caused by microscopic organisms lighting up the waves.

September 6th / Day 249

Mount Everest grows about 4 millimeters each year due to tectonic plate movements. This gradual shift pushes the mountain higher into the sky over time.

September 7th / Day 250

Australia is wider than the moon. The continent spans about 4,000 kilometers across, while the diameter of the moon is roughly 3,474 kilometers.

September 8th / Day 251

Norway is home to the world's longest road tunnel. The Lærdal Tunnel stretches over 24.5 kilometers (15.2 miles) and even has rest areas with special lighting to keep drivers alert during the long journey.

September 9th / Day 252

The Dead Sea is the lowest point on Earth, sitting at more than 430 meters below sea level. Its extreme salinity makes it impossible for most marine life to survive.

September 10th / Day 253

There's a small town in Norway called Hell, and in the winter, it literally freezes over. The town's name comes from an old Norse word meaning "overhang" or "cliff cave."

September 11th / Day 254

Nauru, the world's smallest island nation, doesn't have a capital city. The entire country covers just 21 square kilometers, making it so small that it doesn't need an official capital.

September 12th / Day 255

Antarctica is the driest place on Earth. Despite being covered in ice, parts of the continent receive less precipitation than the world's hottest deserts, making it technically a desert.

September 13th / Day 256

In Japan, there's a train station in the middle of nowhere called Seiryu Miharashi Station. It has no entrance or exit and was built purely for passengers to stop and enjoy the scenic view.

September 14th / Day 257

Lake Baikal in Russia is the world's deepest freshwater lake, plunging to a depth of 1,642 meters (5,387 feet). It holds about 20% of the world's unfrozen freshwater supply.

September 15th / Day 258

The Republic of San Marino is the world's oldest sovereign state and constitutional republic, having been founded in A.D. 301. It's completely surrounded by Italy but has retained its independence for over 1,700 years.

September 16th / Day 259

The Great Wall of China isn't a single continuous wall but a series of walls and fortifications built over centuries. Altogether, it stretches for about 21,196 kilometers.

September 17th / Day 260

Libya is home to the hottest recorded temperature on Earth. In 1922, the temperature in the town of Al 'Aziziyah reached a scorching 58°C (136.4°F), though this record is sometimes disputed.

September 18th / Day 261

There's a "door to hell" in Turkmenistan called the Darvaza Gas Crater. This fiery pit has been burning for over 50 years after a drilling accident ignited the natural gas below.

September 19th / Day 262

The Amazon River is home to the "pink river dolphin," one of the few species of freshwater dolphins in the world. These unique creatures can appear bright pink, especially during mating season.

September 20th / Day 263

New Zealand was the first country to give women the right to vote in 1893, leading the way for women's suffrage movements around the world.

September 21st / Day 264

Greenland is the world's largest island, but around 80% of its surface is covered in ice. Despite its name, it's actually one of the coldest places on Earth.

September 22nd / Day 265

Chile is home to the Atacama Desert, the driest non-polar desert in the world. Some parts of the Atacama have never recorded any rainfall in modern history.

September 23rd / Day 266

Singapore is one of only three surviving city-states in the world, along with Monaco and Vatican City. Despite its small size, it's one of the wealthiest countries in the world.

September 24th / Day 267

Bolivia has two capital cities: La Paz (the seat of government) and Sucre (the constitutional capital). La Paz is also the world's highest capital city, sitting at over 3,500 meters (11,500 feet) above sea level.

September 25th / Day 268

The Philippines is made up of more than 7,600 islands, but only about 2,000 of them are inhabited. The country's total coastline is over 36,000 kilometers long.

September 26th / Day 269

The Maldives is the world's flattest country, with its highest point rising just 2.4 meters (7.8 feet) above sea level. The islands are at risk of being submerged due to rising sea levels.

September 27th / Day 270

Venice, Italy, is slowly sinking. The city is built on wooden piles driven into marshland, and it sinks by about 1-2 millimeters each year as the water levels rise.

September 28th / Day 271

The world's largest cave, Sơn Đoòng in Vietnam, is so massive that it contains its own weather system, with clouds and mist forming inside. It's large enough to fit a 40-story skyscraper within its chambers.

September 29th / Day 272

In South Africa, you can find Table Mountain, one of the oldest mountains in the world, estimated to be about 600 million years old. It's also one of the New Seven Wonders of Nature.

September 30th / Day 273

Monaco is the second-smallest country in the world but has the highest population density. It's only 2 square kilometers, yet more than 39,000 people live there—mostly millionaires!

October: Mysteries and Oddities

October brings a spooky twist, diving into the world of mysteries, oddities, and unexplained phenomena. From eerie urban legends to bizarre scientific occurrences, this month is all about the strange and the unknown.

Whether it's ancient civilizations that disappeared without a trace, unexplained natural events, or modern-day mysteries that defy logic, October will keep you on the edge of your seat.

Get ready for a month of curiosity and intrigue as we explore the weirdest and most mysterious facts our world has to offer!

October 1st / Day 274

The Bermuda Triangle, located between Florida, Bermuda, and Puerto Rico, has a reputation for causing ships and planes to mysteriously disappear. While many theories exist, no definitive explanation has ever been proven.

October 2nd / Day 275

In 1518, the residents of Strasbourg, France, experienced a "dancing plague" where people danced uncontrollably for days. Some even danced themselves to death, and to this day, the cause remains unknown.

October 3rd / Day 276

In the early 1900s, a man named Edward Leedskalnin single-handedly built the mysterious Coral Castle in Florida, using giant limestone blocks. He never revealed how he moved and sculpted the massive stones, leading to speculation about ancient or extraterrestrial technology.

October 4th / Day 277

The Voynich Manuscript, a 600-year-old book filled with strange drawings and an undeciphered language, has baffled cryptographers and scholars for centuries. No one has been able to translate its contents or understand its purpose.

October 5th / Day 278

In 1962, nine hikers mysteriously died in Russia's Dyatlov Pass. Their bodies were found under strange circumstances, and to this day, no one knows exactly what happened to them, sparking numerous conspiracy theories.

October 6th / Day 279

In the 1980s, the "Taos Hum" was reported by residents of Taos, New Mexico—a low-frequency humming noise that only certain people could hear. Despite investigations, the source of the hum remains a mystery.

October 7th / Day 280

Oak Island, off the coast of Nova Scotia, has been the site of treasure hunts for over 200 years. The island is rumored to hide buried treasure, but every excavation has ended in failure and strange accidents.

October 8th / Day 281

In 1977, a radio signal from outer space known as the "Wow! Signal" was detected by a radio telescope in Ohio. The signal lasted 72 seconds and has never been explained or repeated.

October 9th / Day 282

The Mary Celeste, a ship found adrift in the Atlantic Ocean in 1872, was completely intact, but its crew had vanished without a trace. The fate of the crew remains one of the greatest maritime mysteries.

October 10th / Day 283

There's a mysterious place in Mexico called "The Zone of Silence" where radio signals and compasses stop working. It's often compared to the Bermuda Triangle, and no scientific explanation has fully explained the phenomenon.

October 11th / Day 284

The mysterious Antikythera Mechanism, discovered in an ancient shipwreck, is often referred to as the world's first computer. Dating back over 2,000 years, its complexity remains baffling, and scientists are still trying to fully understand its purpose.

October 12th / Day 285

In 1974, thousands of blackbirds mysteriously fell from the sky in a small town in Arkansas. To this day, scientists have been unable to provide a definitive explanation for the mass bird death.

October 13th / Day 286

The Nazca Lines in Peru are massive ancient geoglyphs that depict animals, plants, and shapes. The purpose of these enormous designs, visible only from the air, remains a mystery, with theories ranging from astronomical calendars to alien runways.

October 14th / Day 287

In 1980, a strange phenomenon known as "The Great Smog of London" covered the city in a thick fog so toxic that it caused over 4,000 deaths. The exact combination of factors that led to this disaster remains debated.

October 15th / Day 288

The "Phoenix Lights" were a series of unexplained lights that appeared over Phoenix, Arizona, in 1997. Thousands of people witnessed the event, and no official explanation has ever fully debunked theories of extraterrestrial visitation.

October 16th / Day 289

The "D.B. Cooper" case is one of the most famous unsolved crimes in U.S. history. In 1971, a man hijacked a plane, jumped out with a parachute and $200,000 in ransom, and was never seen again, vanishing without a trace.

October 17th / Day 290

In 1959, the United States attempted to build a secret nuclear missile base under the Greenland ice cap, known as "Project Iceworm." The project was abandoned, but some of its tunnels still exist beneath the ice today.

October 18th / Day 291

The Tunguska event in 1908 flattened over 2,000 square kilometers of forest in Siberia, yet no impact crater was ever found. It's believed to have been caused by a meteor exploding in the atmosphere, but the exact cause is still debated.

October 19th / Day 292

In the 15th century, a mysterious disease known as "The Sweating Sickness" swept through England, causing sudden death within hours of symptoms. The illness disappeared as quickly as it came, and its cause remains unknown to this day.

October 20th / Day 293

In the 1930s, a strange hum known as the "Bloop" was detected in the depths of the Pacific Ocean. The noise was louder than a blue whale's call and has never been fully explained, leading some to speculate it could be from a giant, undiscovered sea creature.

October 21st / Day 294

In 1928, amateur pilot Alfred Loewenstein mysteriously vanished mid-flight. He left his private plane to use the restroom, and when the door opened again, he was gone. Despite investigations, no one has ever determined exactly how or why he disappeared.

October 22nd / Day 295

In the 1930s, a series of stone spheres, some weighing up to 16 tons, were discovered in Costa Rica. Carved by an unknown civilization, their purpose and method of creation remain a mystery.

October 23rd / Day 296

The "Wow! Signal" wasn't the only strange sound from space. In 2016, astronomers detected a mysterious, repeating radio signal from a galaxy over 3 billion light-years away. Its origin is still unknown.

October 24th / Day 297

The mystery of the "Somerton Man" has baffled investigators since 1948. A man was found dead on an Australian beach, with no identification and a mysterious note in his pocket that read "Tamám Shud," meaning "ended" or "finished." His identity remains unknown.

October 25th / Day 298

In 1971, a group of scientists discovered a 300-million-year-old fossilized trilobite, with what appeared to be a human shoe print on it. This "out of place artifact" has sparked debates over the possibility of time travel or advanced ancient civilizations.

October 26th / Day 299

In 1989, the "Hessdalen Lights" in Norway began appearing in the sky. These strange lights have been observed and studied for decades, but scientists are still unsure what causes them.

October 27th / Day 300

The Voynich Manuscript isn't the only mysterious book. The "Rohonc Codex," an illustrated manuscript discovered in Hungary, contains an undeciphered language that has stumped scholars since its discovery in the 19th century.

October 28th / Day 301

The "Devil's Footprints" appeared overnight in 1855 in Devon, England. A series of hoof-like prints stretched for over 150 kilometers, and no one has ever explained how they were made or by whom—or what.

October 29th / Day 302

In 1924, the unexplained deaths of nine explorers at Russia's Dyatlov Pass shocked the world. They were found in the snow with strange injuries, and their campsite was abandoned in panic. Theories about their deaths range from a secret military experiment to extraterrestrial involvement.

October 30th / Day 303

In 1994, a village in Wales reported a strange "rain" of jelly-like substance falling from the sky. The phenomenon, known as "star jelly," has been reported around the world for centuries, but its origin remains a mystery.

October 31st / Day 304

The "Black Knight Satellite" is a mysterious object that some believe has been orbiting Earth for over 13,000 years. While most scientists dismiss it as space debris, conspiracy theorists claim it's an ancient alien spacecraft monitoring our planet.

November: Inventions and Discoveries

November is all about human ingenuity and the discoveries that have shaped our world. From groundbreaking inventions to accidental discoveries that changed the course of history, this month will explore the clever ideas and curious minds behind some of the most significant innovations.

Whether it's a life-changing invention or a quirky discovery that happened by chance, November highlights the moments of brilliance that continue to impact our daily lives.

Get ready to be amazed by the inventive spirit and fascinating discoveries that have transformed the world!

November 1st / Day 305

The microwave oven was invented by accident. In 1945, engineer Percy Spencer noticed that a chocolate bar in his pocket melted while he was working with radar equipment, leading him to create the first microwave.

November 2nd / Day 306

Velcro was inspired by nature. Swiss engineer George de Mestral got the idea after noticing how burrs stuck to his dog's fur during a hike. After years of development, Velcro was patented in 1955.

November 3rd / Day 307

The world's first website is still online. Created by Tim Berners-Lee in 1991, it explains the basics of the World Wide Web. It's a humble beginning for the web, which now hosts over 1.5 billion websites.

November 4th / Day 308

The first electric guitar was invented in 1931 by George Beauchamp. His "Frying Pan" guitar revolutionized the music world and gave birth to modern rock 'n' roll.

November 5th / Day 309

Post-it Notes were invented by accident. In 1968, scientist Spencer Silver was trying to develop a strong adhesive but instead created one that stuck lightly to surfaces without leaving residue, leading to the iconic office supply.

November 6th / Day 310

The safety pin was invented by American mechanic Walter Hunt in 1849. He created it in just a few hours to settle a $15 debt and later sold the patent for $400.

November 7th / Day 311

The discovery of penicillin in 1928 by Alexander Fleming was a lucky accident. He left a petri dish of bacteria out overnight, and it was contaminated by mold that killed the bacteria, leading to the creation of the first antibiotic.

November 8th / Day 312

The first photograph ever taken was by French inventor Joseph Nicéphore Niépce in 1826. The image, taken from a window, required an eight-hour exposure time.

November 9th / Day 313

Bubble wrap was originally invented as textured wallpaper in 1957. When that idea failed, its creators repurposed it as protective packaging, which became a worldwide hit.

November 10th / Day 314

The Slinky was invented by naval engineer Richard James in 1943 when he accidentally knocked a tension spring off a shelf and watched it "walk" down. The toy went on to sell millions.

November 11th / Day 315

Superglue was invented by accident in 1942 by Dr. Harry Coover while he was searching for materials to make clear plastic gun sights during World War II. The adhesive stuck to everything it touched, leading to the development of superglue.

November 12th / Day 316

The pacemaker was invented by engineer Wilson Greatbatch in 1956, who was originally working on a heart-recording device. When he used the wrong resistor, the device began emitting regular electrical pulses, leading to the creation of the pacemaker.

November 13th / Day 317

The ballpoint pen was invented by László Bíró in 1938, inspired by watching how newspaper ink dried quickly and didn't smudge. His invention revolutionized writing and is now used by millions worldwide.

November 14th / Day 318

The discovery of X-rays by Wilhelm Conrad Roentgen in 1895 was entirely accidental. He noticed a fluorescent screen glowing in his lab while experimenting with cathode rays, leading to the development of X-ray imaging.

November 15th / Day 319

The first-ever computer bug was a literal bug. In 1947, computer pioneer Grace Hopper found a moth trapped inside a computer relay, causing a malfunction. This incident coined the term "computer bug."

November 16th / Day 320

Dynamite was invented by Alfred Nobel in 1867. He later regretted his invention due to its destructive use, leading him to establish the Nobel Prizes to reward contributions to peace and science.

November 17th / Day 321

The credit card was invented in 1950 by Frank McNamara after he forgot his wallet while dining out. He came up with the idea for a card that could be used instead of cash, leading to the birth of the modern credit system.

November 18th / Day 322

Insulin, a life-saving treatment for diabetes, was discovered in 1921 by Frederick Banting and Charles Best. Their groundbreaking discovery has since saved millions of lives worldwide.

November 19th / Day 323

The Frisbee started as a pie tin. In the 1940s, students at Yale University would toss Frisbie Pie Company tins around for fun, inspiring the creation of the plastic flying disc we know today.

November 20th / Day 324

The stethoscope was invented by French doctor René Laennec in 1816. He was too embarrassed to place his ear directly on a woman's chest to listen to her heart, so he rolled up paper to create the first stethoscope.

November 21st / Day 325

The thermometer was invented by Galileo Galilei in 1593. His device, called a thermoscope, was the first instrument to measure changes in temperature, although it didn't have a scale like modern thermometers.

November 22nd / Day 326

The postage stamp was invented in 1837 by Sir Rowland Hill. His idea to prepay for mail with a small adhesive label revolutionized the postal system and made sending letters much more efficient.

November 23rd / Day 327

The zipper was invented by Whitcomb Judson in 1893. Initially called the "clasp locker," the design was later perfected by Gideon Sundback and became widely used for clothing and accessories.

November 24th / Day 328

Artificial sweeteners were discovered by accident. In 1879, Constantine Fahlberg, a chemist working with coal tar derivatives, forgot to wash his hands before dinner and noticed his bread tasted sweet—leading to the discovery of saccharin.

November 25th / Day 329

The typewriter was invented in 1868 by Christopher Latham Sholes. It's also responsible for the QWERTY keyboard layout we still use today, designed to reduce the likelihood of mechanical jams.

November 26th / Day 330

Penicillin wasn't the only accidental medical discovery. In 1945, Dr. John Cade discovered lithium's effects on bipolar disorder when he tested the compound on guinea pigs, leading to its use in mental health treatments.

November 27th / Day 331

The first safety elevator, which made modern skyscrapers possible, was invented by Elisha Otis in 1852. His device included a brake that would automatically engage if the hoisting ropes failed, making elevators much safer.

November 28th / Day 332

Matches were invented by British chemist John Walker in 1826. He discovered them while trying to create a new explosive compound and found that scraping a stick covered in chemicals across his hearth caused it to ignite.

November 29th / Day 333

The dishwasher was invented by Josephine Cochrane in 1886. Frustrated by how often her fine china got chipped while being hand-washed, she developed a machine that could clean dishes more efficiently without damaging them.

November 30th / Day 334

The barcode was invented in 1951 by Norman Woodland and Bernard Silver. Inspired by Morse code, they developed the modern barcode system, which has since transformed retail and inventory management worldwide.

December: Holidays and Traditions

December is a time of celebration, filled with festive holidays and rich cultural traditions from around the world. This month, we'll explore the fascinating origins, quirky customs, and surprising facts behind the holidays and festivities that make this season so special. From ancient rituals to modern-day celebrations, each tradition has a story to tell.

Whether it's a well-known holiday or a little-known celebration, December is all about the ways we come together to honor the past, present, and future.

Get ready to discover the history and magic behind the world's most cherished traditions!

December 1st / Day 335

The tradition of decorating Christmas trees originated in Germany in the 16th century. Devout Christians would bring trees into their homes and decorate them with candles, apples, and nuts.

December 2nd / Day 336

In Japan, it's become a tradition to eat KFC on Christmas. This unusual custom began in the 1970s after a successful marketing campaign from the fast-food chain, and now millions of Japanese families order KFC for the holiday.

December 3rd / Day 337

The world's largest New Year's celebration is held in Sydney, Australia. Thanks to its time zone, Sydney is one of the first major cities to ring in the new year, with fireworks lighting up the iconic Sydney Harbour Bridge.

December 4th / Day 338

Hanukkah, also known as the Festival of Lights, lasts for eight days to commemorate the rededication of the Holy Temple in Jerusalem. The menorah is lit each night to celebrate the miracle of the oil that burned for eight days.

December 5th / Day 339

In Iceland, the 13 Yule Lads, mischievous pranksters, visit children in the 13 days leading up to Christmas. Each Lad leaves treats for well-behaved kids and plays tricks on the naughty ones.

December 6th / Day 340

In Italy, La Befana is a witch who delivers gifts to children on January 6th, the day of Epiphany. According to legend, she flies on her broomstick, leaving candy for the good kids and coal for the naughty ones.

December 7th / Day 341

Krampus, a half-goat, half-demon figure from Alpine folklore, is the dark counterpart to St. Nicholas. On December 5th, known as Krampusnacht, he punishes naughty children while St. Nicholas rewards the good ones.

December 8th / Day 342

Boxing Day, celebrated on December 26th in the UK and other Commonwealth countries, originally involved giving boxes of gifts or money to servants and tradespeople in gratitude for their services throughout the year.

December 9th / Day 343

The Jewish tradition of eating fried foods during Hanukkah, such as latkes and sufganiyot (jelly-filled doughnuts), symbolizes the miracle of the oil that burned for eight days in the temple.

December 10th / Day 344

In Mexico, Las Posadas is celebrated from December 16th to 24th. This reenactment of Mary and Joseph's search for shelter is marked by processions, music, and piñatas in the shape of a star.

December 11th / Day 345

The origins of mistletoe as a holiday tradition come from ancient Norse mythology. It was considered a symbol of love and friendship, which led to the custom of kissing under the mistletoe during Christmas.

December 12th / Day 346

In Venezuela, it's a Christmas tradition for people in the capital city of Caracas to roller-skate to early morning church services. Streets are often closed to cars so people can skate safely to "Misa de Aguinaldo."

December 13th / Day 347

In Sweden, St. Lucia's Day is celebrated on December 13th to honor the patron saint of light. The eldest daughter in each family dresses in white, wears a wreath of candles on her head, and serves coffee and treats to the family.

December 14th / Day 348

The first New Year's Eve ball drop in Times Square, New York, was in 1907. The original ball was made of iron and wood and weighed 317 kilograms (700 pounds), a far cry from today's glittering high-tech version.

December 15th / Day 349

In Finland, people celebrate Christmas by visiting a sauna. It's considered a sacred space where people can relax and cleanse themselves before the holiday festivities begin.

December 16th / Day 350

The tradition of the Advent calendar originated in Germany in the 19th century. Originally, families would mark each day of December with a chalk line on the door, but the calendar eventually evolved to include small gifts or chocolates.

December 17th / Day 351

In the Philippines, the Giant Lantern Festival is held in December, showcasing massive, intricate lanterns. The festival, known as Ligligan Parul, symbolizes the Star of Bethlehem and draws visitors from around the world.

December 18th / Day 352

On December 23rd, people in Oaxaca, Mexico, celebrate "La Noche de los Rábanos" (Night of the Radishes), where locals carve large radishes into elaborate sculptures and compete for prizes.

December 19th / Day 353

The Yule log tradition originated in Scandinavia, where a large log was burned during the 12 days of Christmas to symbolize warmth and protection through the winter. Today, the Yule log has transformed into a popular dessert.

December 20th / Day 354

In Greece, Christmas boats, rather than trees, are traditionally decorated. This stems from the country's maritime culture, where decorating ships honors seafarers and symbolizes safe voyages.

December 21st / Day 355

The poinsettia, often associated with Christmas, is native to Mexico. It became a holiday symbol in the 16th century, when a girl placed weeds at a church altar, and they blossomed into the bright red plant we know today.

December 22nd / Day 356

In Austria, Christmas Eve is celebrated with "Silent Night." The famous carol was written in 1818 by Franz Xaver Gruber and Joseph Mohr, and it has since become one of the most beloved Christmas songs worldwide.

December 23rd / Day 357

In Catalonia, Spain, families celebrate with "Caga Tió," a wooden log decorated with a face and a red hat. On Christmas Eve, children "feed" the log and then hit it with sticks, hoping it will "poop" out small gifts and candy!

December 24th / Day 358

The Feast of the Seven Fishes is an Italian-American Christmas Eve tradition, featuring a seven-course seafood meal. It's a nod to the Italian practice of abstaining from meat on religious holidays.

December 25th / Day 359

In Ethiopia, Christmas is celebrated on January 7th, according to the Julian calendar. Known as "Gena," the holiday is marked with church services, feasts, and a game similar to hockey played by men and boys.

December 26th / Day 360

Kwanzaa, celebrated from December 26th to January 1st, was created in 1966 by Dr. Maulana Karenga. It's a week-long celebration honoring African heritage and culture, with each day representing one of seven principles, including unity and self-determination.

December 27th / Day 361

In Japan, it's a New Year's tradition to eat soba noodles on December 31st. Known as "Toshikoshi Soba," the dish symbolizes letting go of the past year's hardships and welcoming a fresh start.

December 28th / Day 362

The tradition of lighting fireworks on New Year's Eve dates back to ancient China. Fireworks were believed to ward off evil spirits and bring good luck for the coming year.

December 29th / Day 363

In Colombia, the "Burning of the Old Year" takes place on New Year's Eve. People create life-sized dolls stuffed with fireworks, which they set ablaze at midnight to symbolize the burning away of the old year's misfortunes.

December 30th / Day 364

In Scotland, Hogmanay is celebrated as the biggest New Year's event, with traditions like "first-footing," where the first person to enter a home after midnight brings luck for the new year. The event often includes large bonfires and celebrations that continue into the early hours.

December 31st / Day 365

In Ireland, it's traditional to bang bread against the walls of a home on New Year's Eve to chase away bad luck and evil spirits. This quirky custom is meant to bring good fortune and ensure a prosperous new year!

In Conclusion

And there you have it—365 fantastic facts, one for each day of the year! From the mysteries of space to the quirks of human traditions, this book has taken us on a journey through the fascinating, the strange, and the downright unbelievable corners of our world. It's a reminder that, no matter how much we think we know, there's always something new to discover.

The world is full of wonders, and sometimes the most surprising things are right in front of us, whether it's the food we eat, the places we live, or the history that shaped us. We hope these facts have sparked your curiosity, made you smile, and maybe even inspired you to dig a little deeper into the topics that caught your eye.

As you go forward, remember that each day brings the opportunity for discovery. The world is an amazing place, and whether through a fun fact or a mind-blowing revelation, there's always something waiting to be learned.

Thank you for joining this adventure of knowledge and fun—keep exploring, stay curious, and never stop asking questions!

Discover More with Our Exclusive Book Bundles!

Looking for a daily dose of fun, learning, and inspiration? The **Daily Laugh & Learn Bundle** is your perfect companion! With 4 engaging books, this collection offers everything from brain teasers and quirky questions to hilarious jokes and fascinating facts. **Embark on a year-long journey of fun and learning!**

Daily Laugh and Learn on Amazon

What's In the Collection?

365 Days of Puns and Pains! The Ultimate Bad Joke Book

Get ready for a year's worth of groans and giggles with the **ultimate** bad joke book. From dad jokes to puns that will make you roll your eyes, this book **guarantees laughter** – and maybe even a few facepalms!

Try This Today! 365 Tiny Tasks to Transform Your Life

Ready for a change? This book is packed with **small, manageable tasks** you can do every day to improve your mood, mindset, and life. From kindness challenges to creative exercises, start **transforming your life**—one day at a time.

365 Fantastic Facts! Your Daily Dose of Delightful Discoveries

Feed your curiosity with fun, surprising facts every day. Whether you want to **impress your friends** or just **learn something new**, these facts will leave you with plenty of "Did you know?" moments!

Quirky Questions for Curious Minds! 365 Thought-Provoking Puzzles to Spark Your Imagination

Take your imagination on a wild ride with **quirky, mind-bending questions** designed to make you **think in new and creative ways**. Perfect for family fun or sparking interesting conversations!

Why Grab the Bundle?

- **Fun for Every Day**: Whether it's a quick laugh, a mind-bending riddle, or a fun fact, this bundle will keep you entertained 365 days a year.
- **Boost Your Creativity**: With thought-provoking tasks and quirky questions, you'll challenge your thinking and inspire your imagination.
- **Affordable Learning**: Get all 4 books at a special bundle price and enjoy a year-long journey of fun and learning!

Get Your Copy Today!

Daily Laugh and Learn on Amazon

Ready to add some laughter and learning to your day? **Head to Amazon** and grab the **Daily Laugh & Learn Bundle**. It's the perfect gift for yourself or someone who loves a good challenge – and a good laugh!

Bring Fun, Curiosity, and Growth Into Every Day!

Want a Sneak Preview?

Get Your First Taste of the Daily Laugh and Learn Series!
We've put together an exclusive sneak peek of the entire **Daily Laugh and Learn** series, giving you a whole week's worth of Solving, Trying, Asking, Laughing, and Learning!

To grab your **FREE preview**, simply sign up for our mailing list by scanning the QR code below:

Unlock Your Exclusive Preview Now!

Get ready to laugh, learn, and brighten up every day. And if you love the experience, we'd be thrilled if you could **leave us a review** on Amazon—your feedback makes all the difference!

Claim Your FREE Book!

Yes, you read that right—a **FREE** book, just for you!

When you purchase any book in the **Daily Laugh and Learn** series, you'll unlock the fun with **Riddle Me This! 150 Brain Teasers to Keep You Thinking**. Join Dan Furze as he takes you on a mind-bending journey filled with puzzles that will challenge your critical thinking and keep you entertained every day.

Claim Your FREE Copy of **Riddle Me This!** now and add even more fun to your collection!

Claim your exclusive FREE book!

Love **Riddle Me This**? We'd love to hear from you! Your **review on Amazon** helps others discover the joy of brain teasers while also building a community of curious minds.

Share your thoughts and let your voice be heard!

About the Author

Dan Furze is an author from the UK known for his engaging and diverse range of books that challenge, entertain, and inform.

With varied titles spanning brain teasers, survival guides, culinary adventures, conspiracy theories, and humor, Dan combines his passion for problem-solving, practical skills, and storytelling to captivate a broad audience.

His most popular works include **"Riddle Me This! 150 Brain Teasers to Keep You Thinking"**, **"Survival 101: or How Not To Die In The Wild"**, and **"Mysteries Unmasked: From Ancient Secrets to Modern Myths in Conspiracy Theories"**.

Whether exploring ancient mysteries or mastering digital security, Dan's books offer readers a blend of wit, wisdom, and intrigue, making complex subjects accessible and enjoyable.

When he's not writing, Dan enjoys experimenting with new recipes, learning about unsolved mysteries, and finding the humor in everyday life.

More by Dan Furze on Amazon

Feel free to get into touch with the author at **<u>dan@furze.media</u>** for any enquiries or feedback.

Printed in Great Britain
by Amazon